# Meet
# **Arnold**
# **Schwarzenegger**

## by Thomas Conklin

## A Bullseye Biography

**Random House** 🏠 **New York**

# To Spud and Chester

Photo credits: AP/Wide World Photos, p. 1, 42, 43, 44, 53, 60, 61, 70, 72, 73, 74, 79, 83, 84 (*left*), 85, 98, 101, 106, 107, 108, 110; Liaison: Gamma Liaison, N.Y., 24; Michael Abramson/Liaison, 35; Star File: Conde/Star File, 82, 84 (*right*), 103; Criss/Star File, 9; Lee/Star File, 4; Shaw/Star File, 102; Zuffante/Star File, 47.

A BULLSEYE BOOK PUBLISHED BY RANDOM HOUSE, INC.
Cover design by Fabia Wargin Design and Creative Media Applications, Inc.
Copyright © 1994 by Thomas Conklin
All rights reserved under International and Pan-American Copyright Conventions.
Published in the United States by Random House, Inc., New York, and simultaneously in Canada by Random House of Canada Limited, Toronto.

*Library of Congress Cataloging-in-Publication Data*
Conklin, Thomas, 1960–
Meet Arnold Schwarzenegger / by Thomas Conklin.
   p.   cm. — (A Bullseye biography)
ISBN 0-679-86748-1
1. Schwarzenegger, Arnold—Juvenile literature.   2. Motion picture actors and actresses—United States—Biography—Juvenile literature.   3. Bodybuilders—United States—Biography—Juvenile literature.
[1. Schwarzenegger, Arnold.   2. Actors and actresses.   3. Bodybuilders.]   I. Title.
II. Series.
PN2287.S3368C66  1994
791.43'028'092—dc20
[B]   94-5180

Manufactured in the United States of America   10 9 8 7 6 5 4 3 2 1

# Contents

# 1

# "The Biggest Star in Hollywood"

Times Square, in New York City, is a busy place. It is the main crossroads in one of the biggest cities in the world. Many movies and TV shows have been made there. One of the worst was made back in 1969.

*Hercules Goes Bananas* was the name of the movie. It is also known as *Hercules in New York*, or just plain *Hercules*. The movie tells what happens when the ancient Greek hero Hercules comes to modern New York. "The action never stops," said the movie's press release. "Hercules is chased by beautiful girls...grizzly bears, gangsters, and an angry Zeus hurling thunderbolts." The movie ended with an "uproarious" chariot race through Times Square, said the press release.

The person who wrote the press release was just about the only person who liked the movie. As one critic wrote, the movie had "an uninspired script, feeble dialogue, and poor direction."

But one person in the movie stood out. The actor playing Hercules was over six feet tall. And he weighed 250 pounds of sheer muscle. He went by the name of "Arnold Strong." Mr. Strong, with his huge muscles, certainly looked like Hercules. But he wasn't much of an actor. In fact, his own voice wasn't even used. After the movie was shot, another actor dubbed all of his lines.

Still, anyone could see that Arnold had a

*"Arnold Strong" in his first film,* Hercules Goes Bananas.

great body. And he had something else—a nice smile and a sense of humor—a *charm* that most other huge bodybuilders don't have. It was too bad that his first movie was so awful. No one could ever make a comeback from a movie like *Hercules Goes Bananas.*

Fast-forward twenty-four years. Another movie is being shot in New York's Times Square. This is no *Hercules Goes Bananas*. Hundreds of people are working on the movie. Traffic is stopped as scenes are shot. TV news teams are covering the confusion and excitement. To top it all off, a seventy-five-foot balloon of the movie's star floats over Times Square. The balloon has been made to look like...

"Arnold Strong."

Yes, the star of the silly movie *Hercules Goes Bananas* was now the biggest star in Hollywood. The movie being made was called *Last Action Hero*. And the star was going by his real name—Arnold Schwarzenegger.

Arnold Schwarzenegger's rise is one of the most incredible stories in Hollywood's incredible history. When he began acting, Arnold could barely speak English. His first

A 75-foot-tall Arnold Schwarzenegger balloon towers over
Times Square during the filming of Last Action Hero. After
the 1993 World Trade Center bombing, the bomb in the
balloon's left hand was replaced with a police badge.

movie was one of the worst ever made. No one would have believed that he would become a big star.

But one person knew he would become a star—Arnold himself. "I can zero in on a vision of where I want to be in the future," Arnold has said. "I can see it so clearly in front of me when I daydream that it's almost real."

Like many people, Arnold dreamed of being a movie star. But, unlike most people, Arnold was ready to work to make his dream come true.

And he worked *hard*.

# 2
# Starting Out

Arnold Schwarzenegger learned all about hard work at a very early age. "Every morning at our house we had squats and sit-ups fifteen minutes before breakfast," Arnold has written. "My father used to say, 'First you have to earn your breakfast.'"

Arnold was born on July 30, 1947, in Graz, Austria. His father was named Gustav, and his mother Aurelia. Their last name, Schwarzenegger, means "black plowman."

Austria is a beautiful country. Graz is surrounded by mountains, forests, and roll-

*Arnold as a young schoolboy (front row,
second from the left).*

ing hills. But in the 1940s Austria was also a very poor country. It is just south and east of Germany, and it was one of the first countries that Nazi Germany invaded and took over. World War II left the country and its economy in rubble.

Arnold was the second child in his family. His brother, Meinhard, was born a year before Arnold. Believe it or not, Arnold was a small, sickly child. But he would soon make up for it!

Arnold grew up in Thal, a small town outside of Graz. Gustav Schwarzenegger was chief of police in Thal. Even though he was an important man in the town, Gustav did not have much money. The family did not have indoor plumbing, central heat, or a telephone. And they did not get a refrigerator until Arnold was fourteen years old.

Even though they had so little money, the Schwarzenegger family found ways to have fun. Gustav was a talented musician, and played six instruments. The family often listened as he led the Thal police band in concerts. And every Sunday Arnold and his brother would go with their parents to the theater or a museum. The next day the boys would have to write a ten-page essay on what they had seen.

Arnold and his brother also participated in many sports, including skating, skiing, hiking, soccer, and table tennis. Like most brothers, they were very competitive. "We were only a year apart," Arnold has said. "We tried to outdo each other when it came to sports and school." The brothers went to Hans Gross school in Thal. Arnold's favorite subject was art. He had a great talent for drawing.

Thal was such a small town that it had no movie theater. But Arnold got his first brush with Hollywood at a very early age. When he was six years old, a swimming pool opened in Thal. A man named Johnny Weissmuller was there to dedicate it. Weissmuller was a former swimming champion who had become a big movie star. He was best known for playing Tarzan, "lord of the jungle." No one in Thal could have guessed at that time that tiny six-year-old Arnold Schwarzenegger would one day be an even bigger star than "Tarzan" himself.

Although Arnold's parents were strict, he loved and respected them. "The only thing we didn't have was money," Arnold has said. "I had a lot of attention from my parents, a lot of love, and enough food."

Arnold's mother was a good cook, although the family was so poor they could afford meat only on Sundays. She also kept their simple house spotless. "The household was a full-time occupation," Arnold has said. "I have one of the best mothers anybody could have."

Arnold was a popular boy growing up. He had a great sense of humor and enjoyed playing practical jokes. One of his favorite pastimes was playing cops and robbers with his buddy Freddy Kattner. (Arnold did not care if he played the good guy or the bad guy!) Arnold also loved comic books. His favorite character was a German superhero named Sieguard.

At age eleven, Arnold had an experience that would change his life forever. He saw his first movie, in Graz. Soon he was going into the bigger town to see movies all the time. The movies gave Arnold a look at his future home. He saw Hollywood's version of life in America—and he liked it.

Arnold later recalled, "What I wanted was to be part of the big cause—the big dreamers, the big skyscrapers, the big money, the big action. Everything in the United States was so big."

Arnold loved adventure and action stories. Two of his favorite movie stars were John Wayne and "Tarzan" himself, Johnny Weissmuller. But, more than anything else, Arnold loved Hercules movies. The stars of the Hercules movies were bodybuilders like Reg Park and Steve Reeves. The young Austrian sat through the movies over and over. He admired the powerful muscles on the stars and dreamed about life in America.

But Arnold lived in a small, poor town in Austria. How could he ever hope to make it to America and Hollywood?

# 3

# "Mr. Universe"

"Good evening, my name is Arnold Schwarzenegger. I would like to do bodybuilding."

The men lifting weights, or "pumping iron," at the gym in the Graz Athletic Union did not know the thirteen-year-old boy. And they did not know why he was introducing himself to each of them. In fact, one of them later said that young Arnold reminded him of a traveling salesman!

But Arnold wanted to become a regular in the gym. That night—in 1961—was the first time he ever visited a weight room. "I still remember that first visit to the bodybuilding gym," Arnold later said. "Those guys were huge and brutal...The weight lifters shone with sweat; they were powerful-looking—*Herculean*. And there it was before me—my life, the answer I'd been seeking."

Arnold and his brother Meinhard had been swimming at a local river earlier that day. There, they met Kurt Marnul, a bodybuilder who ran the gym in Graz. Marnul was impressed by the Schwarzenegger boys. He invited them to work out in the gym.

Arnold was thrilled at the offer. He told his parents that he was visiting the gym in order to get in shape for soccer. But that wasn't his real goal. His real goal was to follow in the footsteps of Reg Park and Steve Reeves—bodybuilders who played Hercules.

Although the Hercules legends are thousands of years old, bodybuilding is a fairly new sport. America's first bodybuilding competition was held in New York in 1903. It was sponsored by a man named Bernarr Macfadden, and the winner won a grand total of $1,000.

The next famous bodybuilder was a man named Angelo Siciliano. He changed his name to Charles Atlas and sold courses on "dynamic tension" in magazines and comic books. Thousands of young men paid to learn Atlas's secrets on how to develop muscles without weights and barbells.

Then, in the years after World War II, thousands of people came to Southern California. Bodybuilding became a popular sport on the beaches there. One beach, south of Santa Monica, became known as "Muscle Beach," because so many people pumped iron there!

It is a long way from tiny Thal, Austria, to Muscle Beach. But Arnold wanted more than anything else to make it there one day.

For a while, both Schwarzenegger boys were regulars at the gym in the Graz Athletic Union. But Meinhard soon grew bored with weight lifting and stopped going. Not Arnold. He loved the sport, and he had a clear goal in mind. He wanted to win the European "Mr. Universe" contest—the Super Bowl of bodybuilding.

"Well, I give myself about five years and I will be Mr. Universe," Arnold used to tell his friends at the gym. "We all looked at each other as if to say, 'This boy is crazy,'" one of them remembered.

But no one could deny that Arnold was dedicated to the sport. He trained every spare moment before or after school.

When the gym opened at five in the morning, Arnold would be at the door, waiting to start. Sometimes he trained at night. He would often miss the last bus to Thal, and would walk the four miles back home.

Kurt Marnul, who ran the gym, gave Arnold training tips. "When you train, think of the muscle you are working on and go to the farthest pain barrier," Marnul would say. "Go on until you cry out."

Arnold took the advice. The other bodybuilders were impressed by his dedication. "We all knew that the building could have fallen down, but Arnold would have continued training," one of them said.

Not everyone understood Arnold's love of bodybuilding. His parents thought it was a strange sport. They only let Arnold train three nights a week. So Arnold began to work out on his own in an unheated room at home.

At the age of fifteen, Arnold left school and began working as a carpenter's apprentice. (In Europe, students often begin learning a trade at a young age.) Arnold soon was earning enough money to support his training on his own.

In 1964, Arnold placed second in a body-building contest in Graz. Soon after, he joined the Austrian army for a year. (All young men in Austria had to serve in the army.) For the first time in his life, Arnold had the chance to eat meat every single day. "The meat made my body respond tremendously," Arnold remembers, "because all of a sudden it got all this protein."

A month after he joined the army, Arnold sneaked away to compete in the Junior Mr. Europe contest in Germany. And he won! Arnold had earned his first major body-building victory. He came back to the army camp a hero. But he was sent to the army jail for leaving without permission. Although Arnold spent seven days in jail, he did not regret what he had done.

Now that he had won a major contest, Arnold worked harder than ever in the gym. And he got results. At the age of 18, Arnold

*A young Arnold, lifting weights.*

stood six feet two inches tall, weighed 245 pounds, and had a 57-inch chest and a 34-inch waist.

In 1966 Arnold won the title Mr. Germany. He also won the International Powerlifting Championship and was named the Best Built Man of Europe. He was ready for the big challenge. Arnold went to London to compete in his first Mr. Universe contest.

Arnold dazzled the Mr. Universe audience. "When he came onstage, it was like somebody had turned on all the spotlights," said one person there. "He just lit the stage up." Arnold finished second to bodybuilding superstar Chet Yorton that day. But it was only a matter of time till he won the biggest prize in bodybuilding.

As Arnold left the theater after his first Mr. Universe contest, people crowded around him. They shoved programs at him. Arnold didn't know what was going on.

"Sign them!" a friend said. "They want your autograph!"

"What a feeling that was, to write 'Arnold Schwarzenegger' across the program," Arnold later wrote. "All of a sudden I was a star." Even his parents were now proud of their son. Arnold's mother, Aurelia, polished his trophies and kept them on display in their house.

At the age of nineteen, Arnold was one of the top bodybuilders in the world. He got there through hard work and dedication. Yet, like most other bodybuilders of that time, Arnold had a secret. He used steroids.

Today, we know that steroids are very dangerous drugs. No bodybuilder will admit to taking them. But back in the 1960s many bodybuilders used them. Arnold was no different. Today, Arnold knows that taking steroids is dangerous. He would never use them again, and he tells everyone else not to use them.

After finishing second at the Mr. Universe contest, Arnold moved to Munich, a large city in Germany. He got a job as a trainer in a gym. At the same time, he kept on his own strict training schedule.

Arnold was very popular, and liked to show off with his sense of humor. He still liked to play practical jokes. Once, before a competition, Arnold told a rival that the latest American style was to scream loudly while posing. His rival did just that—making a total fool of himself onstage.

In 1967, Arnold returned to London for the next Mr. Universe contest. This time he won easily. As he stood on the stage in front of the cheering crowd, he tried to take in what he had just done. "There was just no way I could take it all in. It was like confronting something impossible to lift," he later wrote. Arnold kept telling himself, "What is happening right now is the most important moment in your life."

Maybe that's what he told himself. But Arnold told others about his goals outside of the gym. For instance, he became friends with Wag Bennett, who owned a top gym in London. Bennett always asked young bodybuilders what their goals in life were. Most would just say things like, "I want to be Mr. Universe." But not Arnold.

Bennett asked the teenaged Arnold what his goals were. "I want to be the greatest bodybuilder in the world, the greatest bodybuilder of all time, and the richest bodybuilder in the world," Arnold said. "I want to live in the United States and own an apartment block and be a film star. Ultimately I want to be a producer."

Bennett was amazed. But Arnold was determined to make it all happen.

# 4

# On Top of the World

Arnold Schwarzenegger is such a big star in Hollywood that it is easy to forget how successful he was as a bodybuilder. There has never been another one like him. Other bodybuilders call Arnold the "Austrian Oak" because he is so solid and powerful.

From 1969 to 1975, Arnold won the Mr. Universe title five times. He was also named Mr. Olympia—bodybuilding's other big title—six times in a row. In 1975 Arnold retired, saying he "wasn't giving the others a chance." In 1980 he came out of retirement and won the Mr. Olympia title for the seventh time. All together, Arnold has won far more bodybuilding contests than anyone else in history.

Bodybuilding contests may look like beauty contests. But it takes hours and hours of hard work, and even pain, to train for one. Arnold is known for his hard work.

"Arnold sometimes fainted—passed out unconscious—from the strain of a workout," said one buddy who trained with Arnold. "He even threw up. But he just got up again. He had guts and determination."

To Arnold, training for contests was not just hard work. That's because he loved to train. "I was taught that pain and suffering were not obstacles you should even think about," he has said. "You just go through them."

In 1968, all of the pain and training

began to pay off. Arnold was in London, where he had just won his second European Mr. Universe title. He got a call from Joe Weider, who owned many bodybuilding magazines in the United States. Weider asked Arnold if he wanted to compete in the American Mr. Universe contest in Miami. Weider would pay for Arnold to travel there. In exchange, Arnold would appear in Weider's magazines.

Since America was the land of Arnold's dreams, he immediately said yes, he would come. Arnold jumped on board a plane for Miami, bringing nothing but a duffel bag with a few clothes in it. He was excited. He was sure he would be as successful in America as he had been in Europe.

When Arnold walked out onto the stage in Miami, the audience gasped. He was huge. No one in the competition had bigger muscles. But one man, Frank Zane, had a better "cut." (That means his muscles showed more clearly.) When the judges announced the results, Arnold was in second place behind Zane.

"I was stunned," Arnold later said. He was the biggest—but he wasn't the best. Arnold later remembered the words that ran through his head: "I'm away from home, in this strange city, in America, and I'm a loser..." He cried all that night.

Finishing second in his first American contest made Arnold want to succeed even more. And even though Arnold came in second this time, Weider knew that he could still be the greatest bodybuilder of all time. So Weider offered to pay Arnold a salary for one year. In exchange, Arnold would share his training tips with Weider's readers.

Arnold accepted the offer and moved to Santa Monica. He soon found out why bodybuilders flock to Southern California. To him it was a paradise. "The sunshine, the sea air, and the moderate climate made it ideal for maintaining a body like mine," he said. Arnold shared an apartment with his best friend, fellow bodybuilder Franco Columbo, who followed Arnold from Europe.

As soon as he got to California, Arnold began to study hard to learn English. (Years later he would still have an Austrian accent.) Once he was fluent in English, Arnold began taking college classes. In 1978 he received a college degree in business.

Arnold put his studies to use before he got his degree. Many bodybuilding fans got to know him through Weider's magazines. So Arnold started a mail-order business selling books and cassettes on fitness. It was a great success.

Then, in the early 1970s, Arnold and Franco started a bricklaying business called "Pumping Bricks." Arnold used his charm and brains as a salesman to make the business a success. Once a worker Arnold and

Franco had hired put bricks on a patio in a crooked pattern. Franco was afraid that they would have to do the job over. Instead, Arnold talked to the woman who had hired them. He convinced her that crooked bricks was the latest European style. "She was fascinated," Franco remembered. "She said, 'I like it that way. I want it that way.'"

Arnold used most of the money he earned to buy real estate. He bought an apartment building and some other pieces of property. These investments made him a millionaire while he was still in his early twenties.

And, as always, Arnold pumped iron. He won every bodybuilding competition in sight. Famous artists such as Robert Mapplethorpe and Jamie Wyeth photographed and painted him. Less than five years after coming to America, Arnold was the most famous bodybuilder in the world.

Although Arnold was a success, this was not a completely happy time for him. In May

*Arnold keeps an audience spellbound
as he strikes a classic pose.*

1971, his brother Meinhard died in a car wreck in Austria. Then, in December 1972, Arnold's father died of a heart attack. Arnold was crushed. "I knew how much he had done for me," Arnold later said. "My father saw my progress—that I was developing in my sport and was smart in business—but he never saw the full circle."

To this day, Arnold is close to his mother. He often visits her in Austria and pays her way every time she visits his home in California. And Arnold has been a second father to his brother's son, Patrick. Arnold has helped pay for Patrick's education, and has given him a place to stay in America.

Arnold also showed his generosity by helping people outside of his family. As the most famous bodybuilder in the world, he got tons of fan mail. Much of it came from people in prisons. So in the early 1970s, Arnold decided to help them.

Working with the California government, Arnold started a weight-training program for prisoners. "It makes them release some of their negative tension and energy in the gymnasium," Arnold has explained. "And it gives them a better self-image."

By the mid-1970s, Arnold was at the top of his profession. He had arrived in America determined to become the best bodybuilder in the world—and he was. He had dreamed of being a successful businessman—and he was. But even so, Arnold began to grow bored. He knew that one of his dreams was still on hold.

"I was extremely happy as a body-builder," Arnold has said. "But then, all of a sudden—zap!—it's not enough anymore...I wanted to go again for discomfort, to create the old hunger—to get into acting. Because I knew it was going to happen."

# 5

# *Pumping Iron*

As we have seen, Arnold's first movie was *Hercules Goes Bananas*, made in 1969. In that movie, Arnold had billed himself as "Arnold Strong." When he decided to try out for other roles, his friends urged Arnold to continue to use that name. "Schwarzenegger" was too long, too hard to remember, they said. But Arnold refused to use any name other than his own.

"Someday the world is going to know who I am—just by hearing my first name, Arnold," he claimed.

Arnold's second movie role was in 1973. He earned a tiny part in *The Long Goodbye*, a detective story made by director Robert Altman. Altman is a great director, and the movie was a regular Hollywood production—not a low-budget foreign movie like *Hercules*. But the part was not a big leap forward for Arnold. He played a thug and didn't have any lines—all he had to do was stand still and look mean.

It was about this time that Arnold got his first big break in the movies. It came about after he appeared in a book. Arnold was in New York City for a bodybuilding contest, where he met photographer George Butler. Butler was planning to work on a book about bodybuilding with writer Charles Gaines. "It was clear that Arnold was a star," Butler later said. "His presence was just incredible." Butler and Gaines decided to make Arnold the focus of their book.

The book, *Pumping Iron*, came out in 1974. It was filled with pictures of Arnold and was a big success. For the first time, people who were not fans of bodybuilding saw Arnold.

Arnold's next break came in 1975, when he appeared on the TV talk show *The Merv Griffin Show*. Television great Lucille Ball was watching the show, and liked Arnold's charm and sense of humor. So she invited him to appear on her next TV special.

Before the show, Ball had Arnold study acting for a week. When it came time to shoot the scene, she directed it herself. Learning the art of comedy from Lucille Ball was a huge step up from acting in *Hercules Goes Bananas*!

Now things began to happen quickly for Arnold. His friend Charles Gaines had written a novel about bodybuilding called *Stay Hungry*. It was being made into a movie, and

Arnold was given the part of bodybuilder Joe Santo. It was Arnold's first big movie role.

*Stay Hungry* is different from most Arnold Schwarzenegger movies. Arnold does not use any weapons in the movie, because it's a romantic comedy. His greatest challenge was to learn how to play the violin! (The character Arnold plays is a champion bodybuilder and a fiddle player.) The movie was not a big success. But Arnold was seen to be a good young actor.

In January 1977, Arnold won a Golden Globe Award as "the most promising newcomer of 1976" for his performance in *Stay Hungry*. But he wasn't the most famous muscle-man on the screen. In 1976, Sylvester Stallone had his first great success, in *Rocky*. That movie won both the Golden Globe and Academy Awards. It made Stallone one of the biggest stars in Hollywood. Arnold was determined that his turn would come.

*Arnold accepting the 1977 Golden Globe award
for the most promising newcomer of 1976 for
his performance in the film* Stay Hungry.

In the meantime, George Butler had found
producers who wanted to make a movie version of *Pumping Iron*. Who could be the
star? No one else but Arnold.

*Pumping Iron* gives a behind-the-scenes

look at the 1975 Mr. Olympia competition. It was Arnold's last Mr. Olympia competition before he retired from bodybuilding. And of course, he wanted to go out on top. The movie shows Arnold training with and competing against other bodybuilders—and how he used his sense of humor to get the best of them. In the end, Arnold beats his stiffest

*Arnold taking a ballet lesson during the filming of* Pumping Iron.

*Arnold at the premiere of* Pumping Iron.

competition—Lou Ferrigno, who would go on to play the Incredible Hulk on TV.

On January 18, 1977, the movie version of *Pumping Iron* opened in New York. It was an immediate success. *Pumping Iron* gave a fresh, entertaining look at a sport most people knew very little about. "Arnold lights up the film like neon every time he comes on screen," wrote one critic. "His physical power is balanced by great humor and charm."

Later, people would say that Gaines and Butler discovered Arnold Schwarzenegger. Not true, they say. "Arnold is like the Matterhorn," Butler says, comparing Arnold to the famous mountain. "We didn't discover him. We just noticed him first."

"This week, all New York really cares about is Arnold Schwarzenegger," wrote one critic just after *Pumping Iron* opened. "He's everywhere—in all the papers and magazines, all the gossip columns."

Arnold was on his way. In one month, he had been named Hollywood's most promising newcomer and had a hit movie open in New York. Later that year, his autobiography, *Arnold—The Education of a Body-*

*builder*, was published. It became a bestseller.

Arnold was hot. He began to get many more movie offers. So far, Arnold had played Hercules, a thug, a bodybuilder, and himself. What direction would his career take now? "No Tarzan roles for me," Arnold told a reporter. "I want roles in films that express more emotion than swinging around the branches like monkeys."

On August 28, 1977, Arnold went to the Robert F. Kennedy Tennis Tournament in Forest Hills, New York. Since he was a celebrity, Arnold was invited to meet the family who sponsored the event.

The Kennedys are probably the most famous family in America. John Kennedy had been president, of course. One of his brothers, Robert, had been a senator and was running for president when he was killed. Another brother, Ted, has been a

*A happy couple—Arnold and Maria.*

famous senator for more than thirty years. But it wasn't a Kennedy or any of the other rich and powerful guests who caught Arnold's eye that day. It was a young beauty named Maria Shriver.

Maria's mother, Eunice, is a sister of John,

Robert, and Ted Kennedy. Maria's father, Sargent Shriver, had been head of the Peace Corps and ran for vice president in 1972. Maria herself had just graduated from Georgetown University. All of her life she had been surrounded by "the beautiful people"—rich and powerful men and women. But she had never seen anyone like Arnold.

Arnold had had many girlfriends in his life. But no one had yet captured his heart. Maria—dark-haired, educated, and cultured—was much different from the girls he had met while pumping iron on California's beaches.

Maria and her brother, Bobby, invited Arnold to spend a weekend at their family home in Hyannis Port, Massachusetts. Arnold accepted.

Arnold's weekend was a great success. He spoke German with Ted Kennedy and Sargent Shriver. He went for long walks on the beach with Rose Kennedy, Maria's grand-mother. The two of them talked about music, art, and history. But, best of all, Arnold got to know Maria Shriver.

"I was taken with her sense of humor and absolute joy," Arnold later said. "I knew instantly that Maria was the woman for my life. She was so full of life, so very beautiful."

Arnold had just turned thirty years old. He had come to America and reached every one of the goals he had set for himself. On top of that, he had met and fallen in love with one of the most attractive women in America.

But Arnold's success was just beginning.

# 6

# Conan

After *Pumping Iron*, Arnold seemed on the verge of becoming a superstar. But his next movie almost ended his career just as it was getting started.

Arnold was offered a big part in a comedy called *The Villain*. His costars would be Kirk Douglas and Ann-Margret, two of Hollywood's most popular actors. Arnold accepted the role.

*The Villain* makes fun of old westerns. It is the story of a bumbling villain named Cactus Jack, played by Douglas. Cactus Jack rides into a small town in the old West. He is planning to rob the bank. The people in the town ask another visitor in the town, called "The Handsome Stranger," to stop Cactus Jack. Arnold was to play the Handsome Stranger. The movie was made up of comic chases and stunts.

It was also a flop. The jokes were not funny. Arnold's character was a classic "strong, silent" type. That meant he spent most of the movie sitting still with no expression on his face. His appearance, charm, and sense of humor were wasted. Arnold was "a weight on the movie," wrote one critic. Another said that Arnold was not as good an actor as his horse!

Arnold's next movie was more successful. He was cast in a made-for-TV movie, *The Jayne Mansfield Story*. His costar was Loni Anderson. Jayne Mansfield was a blond starlet in the 1950s and 1960s. The movie is told from the point of view of her second husband, a bodybuilder named Mickey Hargitay. Arnold plays Hargitay in the movie and does a very good job. More important, he learned some lessons about being a star by studying Jayne Mansfield's life. She was a talented star who let her talent go to waste.

"I learned that you have to establish yourself in an area where there is no one else," Arnold later said. "Then you have to create a need for yourself, build yourself up."

With his next movies, Arnold would start to "build himself up" as the king of action movies.

Even as he worked hard at acting, Arnold did not forget the sport that had made him a star. Besides acting in movies, Arnold covered bodybuilding events for CBS Sports. Then, in 1980, Arnold surprised the bodybuilding world by coming out of retirement. He won the 1980 Mr. Olympia contest, even

*As head coach of Special Olympics Weight Training, Arnold helps some Special Olympians get in shape (left) and carries the torch at a Special Olympics ceremony in 1991 (right).*

though it had been five years since he had last competed!

Arnold also helped others become fit by lifting weights. Through Maria Shriver, he learned about the Special Olympics. The Kennedy family had started this event, which gives disabled kids the chance to compete in athletic events.

In 1977, Arnold volunteered to be the national weight-training coach to the Special Olympics. He traveled all around the country helping to raise money for weight-training equipment. Since that time, Arnold has personally trained and made friends with hundreds of disabled kids. "Until you have that type of impact on someone's life," he has written, "you have no idea how good it can make you feel."

By the late 1970s, a change had come over the movies. In the early 1970s, serious movies like *The Godfather* and *Chinatown* were popular. Then, in 1977, *Star Wars* came out and broke all box office records. Science fiction and fantasy became all the rage. And Arnold was just the actor to take advantage of the craze.

The first fantasy character Arnold chose to play was Conan the Barbarian. Conan was created by a writer named Robert E. Howard back in 1932. He is a powerful hero who lives in a mythical time when magic and monsters are common. Conan first appeared in "pulp novels." They were called pulp novels because the paper they were printed on was so cheap. But the movie *Conan the Barbarian* would be anything but cheap.

The script was written by Oliver Stone, who later made *Platoon*, *JFK*, and other hit movies. The director was John Milius, who helped write the war movie *Apocalypse Now*. The budget for the movie was a huge $40 million.

Arnold was John Milius's only choice to play Conan. But the movie's producer had his doubts. Wasn't Arnold the guy who had been upstaged by a horse in his last movie? Yes, but he was the best-built man in the world, said Milius. If they didn't give Arnold the part, they would have to turn someone else into another Arnold Schwarzenegger. At last the producer agreed, and Arnold was given the part.

Making *Conan the Barbarian* was one of the biggest challenges of Arnold's career. Director John Milius made sure all of the details were just right. "John wants to bring to the screen as much reality as possible," Arnold later said. "If you're attacked by a vulture, he wants a real vulture."

This meant that filming the movie was very dangerous. But Arnold did not use a stuntman. "In the first scene I had to be attacked by four live wolves," Arnold remembered. "They let the wolves out of the cages too early. I ran back and fell off the rocks and split my back." Fortunately, Arnold was not badly hurt. "It set the tone for the whole movie," Arnold said. "This was going to be fun...but dangerous."

Arnold was right. Before the movie was

done, Arnold was bitten by a camel and run over by horses. And he hurt his knee shooting a scene in a roomful of snakes!

But it was all worth it. When *Conan the Barbarian* came out in 1982, it was a huge hit. It earned almost $10 million in its first week. Overall, it has earned more than $100 million.

Critics, though, did not like the movie. Many thought it was a silly adventure story. "A kiddie fantasy for grown-ups" is how one described it. Other critics made fun of Conan—and Arnold. "He's not given much opportunity to demonstrate anything except his physique," one wrote. "He is about as emotive as a tree trunk."

His fans didn't care. To them, Arnold *was* Conan—the strong, hard warrior from the distant past. In fact, it was difficult to imagine a better character for Arnold to play.

But Arnold soon found one.

# 7

# The Terminator

Once it was clear that *Conan the Barbarian* was a hit, Arnold went to work on a sequel. To prepare, Arnold worked on his sword-fighting. He invited the director of the next movie, Richard Fleischer, to see him swing his sword. "The first day Fleischer came to see me work out, he told me, 'Arnold, could you put on some more muscles?'" Arnold remembered. "I couldn't believe it!" It seems that Arnold—huge as he was—was not big enough to suit Fleischer!

Arnold returned to the gym. He pumped

iron five hours a day for two months. By the time he started work on the movie, Arnold had put on another ten pounds of solid muscle.

*Conan the Destroyer* was the name of the second Conan movie. Arnold's costars were singer Grace Jones and seven-foot-tall basketball star Wilt Chamberlain.

*Conan the Destroyer* was not as violent as the first Conan movie. Parts of it were funny, and the studio hoped it would appeal to a younger audience. It came out in the summer of 1984 and was a success, earning more than $100 million worldwide. Other movies that year, like *Ghostbusters* and *Indiana Jones and the Temple of Doom*, were bigger hits. But Arnold had proven that he was a top action star—and that kids liked him.

On September 16, 1983, Arnold took a break from preparing for *Conan the*

*Arnold causes a scene at the 1992 Republican National Convention in the Houston Astrodome.*

*Destroyer.* He put on a blue and white striped suit and a red tie and went to the Shrine Auditorium in Los Angeles. There, with Maria Shriver at his side, Arnold Schwarzenegger was sworn in as an American citizen.

"I always believed in shooting for the top," Arnold told reporters that day. "Becoming an American is like becoming a member of a winning team."

Arnold is a well-known patriotic supporter of the United States. "When I came to America, it was like heaven," he has said. "All of the great things have happened to me since I came here."

Arnold is a conservative Republican. Although Maria Shriver comes from a family of famous Democrats, Arnold makes no secret of his political views. He strongly supported President Ronald Reagan, and went to the 1984 Republican convention. Four

*Arnold attends the 1991 dedication of the Ronald Reagan Presidential Library in California.*

years later, Arnold worked to help elect George Bush.

Maria respects Arnold's conservative views. "Arnold has specific opinions on issues that he really thinks through and supports by facts," she has said.

By early 1984, Arnold was a top box office draw. His movies had begun to make a lot of money. Producers sent him dozens of scripts, hoping he would agree to star in their movies. One 122-page script landed on Arnold's desk. It was written by a talented young writer and director named James Cameron. Its title: *The Terminator*.

*The Terminator* is the story of a robot from the future sent back in time to kill a young woman. A human hero from the future follows closely behind. The hero and the robot battle to the death in modern Los Angeles.

"I have read a lot of action scripts, and this definitely was one of the best," Arnold said. Strangely enough, Cameron sent the script to Arnold to see if he was interested in playing the human hero. Cameron had ex-football star O. J. Simpson in mind for the role of the Terminator. Arnold definitely was interested—but not in playing the hero.

"I knew that I wanted to play the part of the Terminator as soon as I started reading," he says. In all of his other roles, Arnold had played the hero. Here was a chance to show another side of his acting skills. Cameron agreed that it was a good idea, and Arnold got the part.

Arnold did not "pump up" for his role as the lean, mean killing machine. In fact, he later joked that it was a big breakthrough for him. For the first time, he kept his shirt on for most of a movie! *The Terminator* was indeed a big breakthrough for Arnold. It was a bloody action movie, like the Conan movies. But it was also an intelligent science fiction story.

Critics and audiences agreed that *The Terminator* was a success. "Thrill-packed," "fast and furious," "astounding," they wrote. *Time* magazine named it one of the ten best movies of the year. Audiences loved its interesting story, its thrilling chases, and its star—Arnold.

Some critics who liked the movie still thought Arnold was not much of an actor. ("As a robot, Arnold Schwarzenegger has at last found a role suited to his talents," one joked.) Arnold defended himself. "It's much more challenging to play a robot than a human," he told *People* magazine. Even though he had few lines, Arnold is the star of the movie. One of his lines, "I'll be back," has become a popular saying.

Arnold knew that he had turned a corner

with *The Terminator*. Sure, he would not be playing Hamlet anytime soon. But he would not have to be simply a muscle-man anymore. "After I did *The Terminator*...people then sent a variety of different kinds of scripts," Arnold later said. "All in the action-adventure genre, but they were not all muscle movies or Viking movies or pirate movies or anything like that..."

Still, some people thought that the idea of Arnold Schwarzenegger being an actor was a joke. Whether or not he kept his shirt on, Arnold still was a muscle-man—one with a thick Austrian accent. But Arnold didn't care what others thought. He told an interviewer, "As far as I'm concerned, I will, in a few years, be where the top people are now, whether it's Eastwood, Stallone, or Redford—anyone who makes the top salary. I feel absolutely certain that's where I will be."

# 8

# The King of Action Movies

In the summer of 1985, Arnold and Maria Shriver sat in a theater in Hollywood. They were watching his latest movie. As Arnold remembered it, Maria turned to him as the movie ended, and said, "If this movie doesn't ruin your career in two seconds, then you have tremendous staying power in this town."

The movie was *Red Sonja*, Arnold's next movie after *The Terminator*. It was one of the biggest flops ever. *Red Sonja* was based on characters created by Robert E. Howard, who wrote the Conan stories.

Arnold had agreed to play a small part in it as a favor to the producers of the Conan movies. When *Red Sonja* was done, every last scene Arnold shot was used, and he was billed as a star. But despite Arnold's name above the title, the terrible movie was a box office dud.

"I was happy that it did as bad as it did," Arnold said, "because people had no chance to see the movie!"

Even though *Red Sonja* came and went quickly that summer, Arnold was once more in the news. On August 10, 1985, he and Maria announced their engagement to be married. Then, a few weeks later, Maria was made the news anchor on *CBS Morning News*. Successful and attractive, Maria and Arnold were seen as the model American couple.

Arnold's next movie after *Red Sonja* was *Commando*. *Commando* was a violent adventure movie. But along with all of the bullets, chases, and fights, the movie also called on Arnold to *act*.

In *Commando*, Arnold plays Colonel John Matrix. Matrix is a weapons expert and commando who has retired from the military to raise his young daughter. When a group of terrorists kidnap his daughter, Matrix must go back into action to save her. Throughout the story, Matrix shows not only a talent for killing the bad guys, but a sharp sense of humor.

Arnold impressed his fellow actors with his skills. "Arnold is a movie star," said costar Rae Dawn Chong. "He's smart, beautiful to look at, and more talented than people realize."

As usual, Arnold did most of his own stunts. In one scene John Matrix hangs on to the landing gear of an airplane as it zips down the runway at 65 miles per hour. "If I had made a mistake, I would have been crushed by the wheel," Arnold later said. "The danger was real!"

"There's nobody else but Arnold who could have done what he did," director Mark Lester claimed. "I've made fifteen pictures, and he's the only actor who could have done the kind of action that we've done."

*Commando* opened to good reviews. Critics saw that Arnold was now a much better actor than he had been in his Conan days. Arnold's fans also liked the new movie, and made *Commando* one of the biggest hits of the year.

"I'm achieving the kind of success I always knew I would," Arnold said. *Commando* was a financial success, and for the first time Arnold was praised as an actor. "I want to keep making movies the world loves to see," he said.

And he did. His next movie, *Raw Deal*,

*Arnold in a scene from* Raw Deal.

was a real change for Arnold. It was a gangster movie. *Raw Deal* presented Arnold as an
undercover FBI agent up against the Mafia
in Chicago. In one part of the movie, Arnold
wore a three-piece suit and tie—quite a

change from his loincloth-and-sandals days as Conan!

In his next movie, *Predator*, Arnold returned to science fiction. Arnold plays Major Dutch Schaefer, a guerrilla fighter leading a team of soldiers on a mission in Central America. While prowling through the jungle, the men are attacked by a terrifying creature from outer space. The creature, armed with powerful weapons and able to become invisible, is killing the men for the fun of it. Soon, only Major Schaefer is left to battle—and defeat—the creature.

"I took more abuse in *Predator* than I did in *Conan the Barbarian*," Arnold later said. "I fell down that forty-foot waterfall and swam in this ice-cold water for days and for weeks was covered in mud...It was terrible."

But the hard work was worth it. When *Predator* was released in June 1987, it shot to the top of the box office charts. All in all, it made more than twice as much as *The Terminator*—Arnold's first science fiction thriller.

In April 1986, Arnold took time off from filming *Predator*. He traveled to Hyannis Port for a new starring role—happy husband.

Arnold and Maria were married on April 26. All of Arnold's family and friends were at the church. His mother was there. Arnold's best man was his old bodybuilding buddy, Franco Columbo. Dozens of his body-

*Arnold on the night before his wedding to Maria.*

*Arnold and Maria pose after their 1986 wedding.*

building friends and rivals were there to celebrate Arnold's marriage. So were many show business celebrities—like Grace Jones and artist Andy Warhol.

The wedding was the social event of the year. Maria wore a stunning Dior gown. The wedding cake stood seven feet tall and weighed 425 pounds. Most of the guests agreed with Maria's aunt Ethel, who said, "It

*Arnold and Maria celebrate the 100th birthday of Maria's grandmother, Rose Kennedy.*

was the most beautiful wedding ceremony I've ever been to in my life."

Arnold's next movie was *The Running Man*. It was another science fiction story, set in the future after a huge corporation has taken over the world. Arnold plays Ben Richards, an innocent policeman blamed for killing a group of poor people rioting against the corporation. As punishment, Richards is forced to appear on *The Running Man*, a TV game show where cartoonish "stalkers"—performers like present-day wrestling stars—hunt down and kill people. Of course, Richards survives and manages to get rid of the evil corporation as well.

*The Running Man* is based on a novel by the famous writer Stephen King. The movie is full of action and humor. It also had Arnold's best performance at that point. "I am extremely delighted," Arnold said, just before the movie opened. "*The Running Man* is going to be a smash."

Arnold was right. It made almost $35 million in its first three weeks. Soon after, Arnold was given the 1987 Star of the Year Award by the National Association of Theater Owners. According to them, he was the top movie superstar in the world.

Arnold's next film, *Red Heat*, made history. It was the first American movie to have scenes shot in Moscow. Arnold played a Russian police detective, and worked hard to prepare for the role. He lost ten pounds in order to look more like a lean, tough Russian cop. And he spent three months studying a new language—the first twenty pages of the script were in Russian!

*Red Heat* was not as big a hit as *Predator* or *The Running Man*. In fact, for a change, critics seemed to like the movie more than Arnold's fans did. The critics also liked Arnold's performance as a tough Russian who learns to be more gentle and humane.

Would Arnold return to science fiction in his next movie? Arnold gave a hint in an interview after *Red Heat*. "Certainly people don't want to see the same exact movie again," he said. "But they don't mind seeing the same *type* of movie."

So far, Arnold had shown that he was best in science fiction and comedy. So he decided to combine both types of story in his next movie.

# 9

# The "Granite Teddy Bear"

"Schwarzenegger seems happy to laugh at himself," wrote one critic. "He's like a granite teddy bear."

The critic was writing about *Raw Deal*—a violent movie with only a few laughs thrown in. But Arnold's sense of humor showed—even in a tough gangster movie. So, after Arnold's amazing success in 1987 and 1988, he decided to make a comedy.

Back in 1984, Arnold had met Ivan Reitman, director of *Ghostbusters*. "I would love to do a movie with you sometime," Arnold said. Reitman never forgot what Arnold had said. Later, after Arnold had become the top star in Hollywood, the two met for lunch. Reitman began to describe his idea for an Arnold Schwarzenegger movie.

Suppose two test-tube babies were born as part of a science experiment, Reitman said. Suppose that one baby got all of the intelligence, good looks, and honesty. The other was a runt, and was placed in an orphanage. Thirty-five years later the tall, handsome, intelligent brother seeks out his twin...

"Halfway into my pitch," Reitman said, "Arnold said, 'When do we start?'"

And so *Twins* was born.

Making *Twins* was physically easy for Arnold. (At least he didn't have to fight wolves or ride down runways holding on to an airplane's wheels!) But it was a great acting challenge. Arnold had to play a man who

*Arnold and Maria
out on the town.*

was as innocent as a child, but also highly intelligent. He also falls in love with a woman. "In my last five or six movies, my love relationship was basically with guns..." Arnold later said. "*Twins* was for me a learning experience all the way through."

Reitman knew that Arnold could handle the part. "The key...was to let him be absolutely open," Reitman said. "To strip all of the acting away and let the real person come through."

When the movie was finished, Arnold was happy with the results. "I think *Twins* is going to have a surprising impact," he told an interviewer. "And it's going to be good for my career, because then I can do more of the movies I would like to do."

Reitman agreed. He told Maria, "People will finally understand why you married Arnold."

But the producers were worried. They wondered if the "hard-core Arnold fans"—people who loved his action movies—would like seeing Arnold in a comedy. "It made everyone feel uncomfortable..." Arnold remembered. "I really enjoyed doing comedy, but there would always be confrontations with the directors, the studios. 'Naw, naw, naw. What we want you to do is be a tough guy.'"

Arnold was right, and the producers were wrong. *Twins* opened on December 9, 1988, and was a huge hit. His action fans liked the movie—and so did other people who would never think of going to see *Raw Deal* or *Commando*. In less than one month, *Twins* made more than $100 million!

Looking back, it's easy to see that Arnold had prepared his fans for a comedy like *Twins*. His first big success as an actor had been playing the grim, serious Conan. In every one of his movies since, Arnold had pushed himself a little bit more as an actor.

"I always felt it was best to build up stock with an audience out there that will always go see your movies…" Arnold has explained. "But that doesn't mean you can't add on every time ten percent of new stuff and gradually make them see a new side of you."

One year after *Twins*, the world saw another side of Arnold—he became a loving father. Katherine Eunice Schwarzenegger, Arnold

*Katherine Eunice Schwarzenegger with her parents.*

and Maria's first child, was born on December 13, 1989, in Los Angeles.

Arnold was thrilled. Before he and Maria married, he used to joke, "If we marry and have kids, with her body and my mind they'll have some real winners in the family." Now, with Katherine, the family of "Schwarzenshrivers" was on its way.

Of course, Arnold had already shown that he likes kids. For example, he still worked closely with the Special Olympics. In December of 1988, Arnold held a special premiere of *Twins* to raise money for the organization. The audience included President-elect George Bush, whom Arnold had supported in the election that year.

In January 1990, President Bush gave Arnold a chance to take his message about physical fitness to *all* of the kids in America. He made Arnold chairman of the President's

*Arnold receives an award from President George Bush for his contribution to the Simon Wiesenthal Center. The Center is dedicated to the study of the Holocaust.*

Council on Physical Fitness and Sports.

This was about the greatest honor Arnold could have hoped for. It was twenty-two years since he had first come to America. Back then, he had been an unknown twenty-year-old. All he had then were the clothes in his gym bag and high hopes. Now he was the

*Arnold and Governor Zell Miller of Georgia talk to children at the Charles Drew Elementary School in Atlanta (left). Arnold leads students in calisthenics at Jose Clemente Orozco Academy in Chicago (right).*

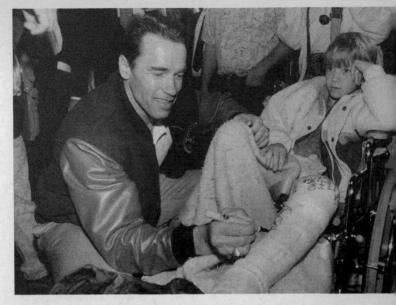

*As part of his job with the President's Council on Physical Fitness and Sports, Arnold visited schools in all fifty states. Here he signs the cast of Chris Hess in a Maryland school.*

biggest star in Hollywood—and the government's spokesperson on a very important issue.

"I owe America," Arnold said when he took on the job as chairman. "Here's my chance to give something back."

# 10

# Three Home Runs

The movies you see on the screen are only one part of the work done in Hollywood. Hundreds of movie scripts are bought by producers and "put into development." That means the producers look for stars and directors to work on the movie. It costs millions of dollars to make a movie. Producers want to know a movie has a good chance of being a success before they make it. That means finding popular stars. Some great scripts never get made into movies because the right star is not found to act in them.

*Total Recall* seemed certain to be one of those scripts.

Way back in 1974, producer Ron Shusett and writer Dan O'Bannon met to talk about ideas for movies. One of their ideas was for a movie about killer space aliens. The other was to make a movie from a science fiction short story, "We Can Remember It for You Wholesale." (The story was by Philip K. Dick, a well-known writer.) Shusett and O'Bannon decided the story was too complicated to make a good movie. So they worked on the alien idea. They called their script *Alien*.

*Alien* was a huge hit in 1979, at the beginning of the science fiction boom. The next year, the movie *Blade Runner* came out. *Blade Runner* was based on another story by Philip K. Dick. Seeing how good *Blade Runner* was, Shusett and O'Bannon thought back to "We Can Remember It for You Wholesale." They decided to work on a script based on it.

The result was the script for *Total Recall*. Everyone who read it agreed that it was a fabulous script. But no one wanted to take the risk of making it. The story was just too complicated. A few stars thought about taking on the project—including Patrick Swayze, Richard Dreyfuss, and "Superman" Christopher Reeve. But no one came through.

Then Arnold read *Total Recall*.

"I knew the script was a good one," Arnold has said. "I could not put it down. I thought there was a lot I could do with the movie."

Fresh from his success in *Twins*, Arnold wanted to return to a straight science fiction thriller. He would make *Total Recall*.

It was the perfect story for him at that point in his career. *Total Recall* is set in 2084. Earth is run by dictators, who have huge mining operations on Mars. Arnold plays Douglas Quaid, a quiet, gentle man—much like his character Julius in *Twins*.

Over time, Quaid discovers that he is not really a construction worker, as he had thought. He is a secret agent with an implanted false memory. Quaid heads to Mars, where he has a series of thrilling—and extremely violent—adventures.

Arnold asked Paul Verhoeven to direct the movie. Verhoeven was, like Arnold, born and raised in Europe. In 1987 he had his first big success in America with the science fiction movie *Robocop*. Arnold thought he would be a perfect director for *Total Recall*. And Verhoeven was eager to work with Arnold.

"Arnold is great," Verhoeven has said. "He's one of the few people in my life that I really admire...He's also done a really good job acting."

It took six months and more than three hundred people working full-time to make *Total Recall*. By the time it was finished, the movie cost more than $73 million. (Arnold himself was paid $10 million to star in the movie!) The special effects alone took months of work and cost millions of dollars. In short, *Total Recall* was a huge gamble.

The gamble paid off. The movie was released in June 1990 and was an instant hit. Critics praised Arnold's performance. And his fans flocked to see Arnold back in an adventure thriller. It was his biggest hit up to that point.

But Arnold was not able to let the success go to his head. He called his mother to brag when *Total Recall* made over $100 million. "She replied, 'Let me tell you, your uncle yesterday came to visit me here, and he brought me all these wonderful flowers,'" Arnold remembered. Arnold had had his greatest hit, but his mother still reminded him of the important things—family, and caring for others.

Arnold's next movie was one that even his mother could love. *Kindergarten Cop* was about a tough policeman who goes undercover as a kindergarten teacher. He is able to deal with tough criminals—but a class of five-year-olds is more than he can handle.

In *Kindergarten Cop*, Arnold worked again with Ivan Reitman, the director of *Twins*. Together, he and Arnold visited schools to find kids to play Arnold's pupils. As he visited real kindergartens, Arnold learned that his movies—even the most violent ones—were popular with kids.

"I was in a state of shock," Arnold recalled. "Ivan would ask the kids, 'Does anyone know who this is?' And they would all go, 'Yeah! *Predator! Terminator! Twins!*'"

Acting with kids was a new experience for Arnold—one he enjoyed. "Those children were incredible," he said. "They would make drawings for you and give you little photographs…You really looked forward to going to the set and seeing all these kids and having laughs."

Arnold's fondness for the kids comes across on screen. "Schwarzenegger…is touchingly sincere," wrote critic Roger Ebert. When it was released in December 1990, *Kindergarten Cop* was an immediate success. It wound up making more than $85 million. *People* magazine named it one of the year's ten best movies.

With the tremendous success of *Kindergarten Cop*, Arnold completed the most successful year any movie star ever had. All together, the three movies Arnold starred in during the twelve months from December 1989 to December 1990 made more than $300 million at the box office.

When *Red Sonja* came out in 1985, Arnold was laughed at. People said he was a muscle-man with no talent as an actor. Five years later, he put out *Twins*, *Total Recall*, and *Kindergarten Cop*—three hits like none in Hollywood history.

What more could Arnold possibly do?

# II

# He's Back!

In 1990, it had been six years since Arnold had made *The Terminator*. In those years, Arnold had been busy becoming the biggest star in Hollywood. But he wasn't the only person who worked on *The Terminator* to hit it big. Costar Linda Hamilton had later starred in the TV show *Beauty and the Beast*. And director James Cameron had gone on to make *Aliens*, the popular sequel to *Alien*.

"I've been offered a lot of money to do sequels to my other films, like *Predator* and *Commando*," Arnold told *US* magazine.

"But the only one I wanted to do was *The Terminator*. I also made it clear that I wouldn't do it without Jim Cameron."

Was Cameron interested in making a sequel to Arnold's "breakthrough" movie? "He's a machine," Cameron said about the Terminator. "Machines are mass-produced, so there might be another one in the warehouse..."

In October 1990, filming began on the sequel to *The Terminator*. When Arnold read the script, he was surprised. His character was more or less the same in this story—with one big difference. This time he was the good guy!

The sequel was called *Terminator 2: Judgment Day*, but most people call it *T2*. In this story, a killer robot from the future comes back to kill John Connor, the son of the first movie's heroine. This second robot is a "newer" model of Terminator. Instead of being a huge, powerful robot, it is made of liquid metal. It can change its shape by itself. One of the older Terminators is also sent back in time—to protect John Connor. The "good" Terminator was played by Arnold.

This plot gave Arnold a chance to really show his acting skills. At the beginning of the movie, he is the same cold, unfeeling robot he was in the first movie. But he makes friends with John Connor. The boy teaches the Terminator about human emotions.

In the first movie, Arnold's character had a total of seventeen lines to speak. In *T2*, the Terminator learns to communicate with humans. John Connor even teaches him slang, such as "No problemo" and "Hasta la vista, baby."

Linda Hamilton returned to play Sarah Connor, the same character she played in the first movie. Cameron thought about hiring rock star Billy Idol to play the bad Terminator, but he hired actor Robert Patrick instead. Twelve-year-old Eddie Furlong was hired to play John Connor.

"The film is much bigger than the first one," Arnold said, "and the experience making it has been very intense."

"Intense" is just the word to describe the action in *T2*. Scenes in the movie were shot in and around Los Angeles, in the Mojave desert, and in an abandoned steel mill in Florida. In one scene, Arnold drives a motorcycle down drainage ditches in Los Angeles as a huge semi-truck chases him. In another scene, Arnold's character blows up a building. Cameron and his crew actually blew up a real building, while eight movie cameras recorded the scene!

Motorcycle and truck chases and exploding buildings were just the beginning. By the time it was finished, *T2* was the most expensive movie ever made. Many of the special

*Arnold holds the People's Choice Award won by* Terminator 2: Judgment Day.

effects—such as the liquid-metal robot—had to be invented from scratch. And the cast was expensive—Arnold alone was paid a $12 million Gulf Stream jet for starring in the movie. All together, the producers spent $94 million on the movie. Could *T2* possibly make it all back?

As Arnold's Terminator said: "No problemo." When *T2* was released on July 3, 1991, it zoomed to the top of the box office charts. It earned an incredible $70 million in one week. By the end of the year, *T2* had earned $240 million, and was on its way to becoming one of the biggest hits in Hollywood history.

Critics loved the movie—and Arnold, too. His acting was "impressive, hilarious, almost touching," one critic wrote. *T2* went on to win five Academy Awards for special effects and makeup.

Will there be more *Terminator* movies? Don't be surprised if there are. "I don't want to leave the magic of the *Terminator* movies behind," Arnold has said, "and who says we have to?"

# 12

# "The Greatest Thrill of All"

In his next movie, Arnold would take his biggest risk yet. So far, all of his movies had fallen into one of three categories: science fiction/fantasy, action-adventure, or comedy. In *Last Action Hero*, Arnold would mix all three styles. The movie would be a fantasy, it would make fun of action movies, and it would be filled with the thrills and adventures found in action movies.

*Last Action Hero* tells what happens when a real boy enters the world of an action

*Arnold and Maria stroll through New York City's Times Square on the first evening of filming* Last Action Hero.

movie and brings his favorite action hero— played by Arnold—back into the real world. The original script was written by two young men right out of college, Zak Penn and Adam Leff.

Although the script needed work, Arnold liked the story. He had had the same fantasy when he was a boy watching adventure movies back in Graz. Arnold used to imagine he was on the screen, helping John Wayne

*Arnold as Jack Slater,
in* Last Action Hero.

beat the bad guys. Early in 1992, he decided to make *Last Action Hero*.

Making the movie was very difficult. Many different writers were hired to work on the script, which delayed the shooting. And part of the movie was shot in Los Angeles neighborhoods that had been destroyed in the April 1992 riots. It took time for the movie company to rebuild many buildings, which they donated to neighborhood groups when the movie was finished.

Arnold had to put up with a lot while making *Last Action Hero*. In one scene, his character is stuck in the La Brea tar pits—the oily swamps outside of Los Angeles. The scene was shot using a black goop made from Oreo cookie dough. Arnold spent many hours stuck in the stuff!

Then, early in 1993, the movie company came to New York City to shoot some scenes. (This was when the huge balloon figure of Arnold was put up in Times Square.) But the biggest blizzard of the decade hit the city in the middle of filming. That delayed things even more. The movie

*Arnold and co-star Austin O'Brien at the premiere party for* Last Action Hero.

was scheduled to come out in June 1993, and Arnold was filming action scenes right up to the last minute. By the time is was finished, *Last Action Hero* was every bit as expensive as *T2* had been.

But unlike *T2*, *Last Action Hero* would have a lot of competition. Steven Spielberg's dinosaur epic, *Jurassic Park*, was coming out at the same time as *Last Action Hero*. Who would be more popular—Arnold or the dinosaurs? Everyone in Hollywood waited to see.

The producers of *Last Action Hero* did everything they could to promote the movie. They worked with toy-makers and fast-food companies. They even offered NASA $500,000 to put Arnold's name and picture on a rocket being launched into space!

Unfortunately, none of this worked. *Last Action Hero* was Arnold's biggest disappointment since *Red Sonja*. His fans didn't know what to make of the fantasy/comedy/adventure. Most critics were very nasty in their reviews. And *Jurassic Park* was the strongest competition any movie could possibly face. By the end of the year, *Jurassic Park* was the biggest hit in Hollywood history—while *Last Action Hero* barely made enough money to cover its costs.

What is next for Arnold? "Someday I would like to do a romantic comedy," he has said. "I would also like to do a hard-core western and a good, traditional war movie—any of those things would be appealing."

Arnold is still just about the hottest star in Hollywood. He has been offered many different roles, in projects ranging from a violent war story called *Sergeant Rock* to a movie based on the children's book *Curious George*. As this is being written, Arnold is working on a movie called *True Lies* with director James Cameron, who made the *Terminator* movies. There are also rumors that Arnold is planning a movie called *Crusades* with Paul Verhoeven—who made *Total Recall*—and another called *Junior,* costarring Danny DeVito and directed by Ivan Reitman.

Besides acting, Arnold has plenty to keep him busy. He owns a number of restaurants—including a chain called Planet Hollywood, which he owns along with fellow movie stars Sylvester Stallone and Bruce Willis.

Arnold has discovered that he likes to

*Bruce Willis, Arnold, and Sylvester Stallone pose at the opening of their nightclub, Planet Hollywood, in 1991.*

*Arnold and Sylvester Stallone dance for the cameras at a film festival in France.*

direct movies, too. He has directed two made-for-TV projects—*The Switch*, a short horror story, and *Christmas in Connecticut*, a full-length movie. "I felt ecstatic," Arnold said, telling what it was like to direct. "It was something I never expected. To work with actors and mold a scene. It's wild." Arnold also plans to direct feature films.

*Arnold and Maria enjoy a New York Knicks game in 1993.*

Although it's been almost fifteen years since he was in a bodybuilding contest, Arnold still keeps in fantastic shape. He works out at least one hour every day, lifting weights and doing some cardiovascular exercise, such as running or bicycle riding. He has also kept up his ties with bodybuilding, sponsoring a competition called the Arnold Classic.

Beside movies, business, and bodybuilding, Arnold finds time for many hobbies. He loves horseback riding, collecting fine art and antiques, and going to sporting events and classical music concerts. But Arnold has his wilder side as well. He likes to ride his purple Harley-Davidson motorcycle, and he often takes his kids for rides in his "Humvee"—a huge army vehicle.

And, of course, his family takes up a lot of Arnold's time. He and Maria now have three children—Katherine Eunice, Christina Aurelia, and Patrick. "I love being a dad," Arnold says. "For me, it's the greatest thrill of all."

It seems as though Arnold lives the perfect life. He has all of the good things anyone could hope for—fame, fortune, and a happy family. But he started his life very poor, in a small, unheated house. Arnold worked hard, and took many chances, to get where he is today.

"Good things don't happen by coincidence," Arnold says. "Every dream carries

*Arnold gets his star on the Hollywood Walk of Fame, 1987.*

with it certain risks, especially the risk of failure. If you take the risk and fail, you must try again and again."

Arnold—athlete, movie star, happy family man—has worked hard, taken big risks, and earned every bit of his success.

THOMAS CONKLIN is the author of two other biographies for young readers: *Muhammad Ali: The Fight for Respect* and *Meet Steven Spielberg*. A children's book editor, he lives in Maplewood, New Jersey, with his wife, two dogs, and two cats.

# Bullseye Biographies